D1161163

Magnus O'Meere, Mind Pioneer

Pioneered by Kristin Pierce

Pictures by Mar Fandos

Inner Compass
Books.com

When Magnus O'Meere was a bright little lad,
He opened a gift from his favourite granddad.

Sparking epic ideas, at the ripe age of five,
This hand-me-down gift made him feel so alive.

He'd uncovered a passion—it was crystal clear.
He courageously tinkered without any fear.
He got wrapped in ideas, devoted his time,
And saved his allowance to use every dime...

On trinkets and tracks, on jacks and jet packs,
Toy motors, grand gadgets, and Nana's knickknacks.
A stockpile of parts to upgrade and concoct
Each masterpiece that his mind had unlocked...

Like a hydration helmet that let him take sips,
And a nifty note holster that attached to his hips.

He'd record inspiration; incubate, then unlatch
The glorious gadgets that were ready to hatch.

His creations grew wild, as young Magnus did, too,
And his parents suggested to try something new.

But it didn't stop him—unaffected, amid
His parents' concern for a well-rounded kid.

'Cause, Magnus O'Meere, he was head over heels
For building new dreams with gears, rackets, and reels.

And that's how it went till one day in grade three,
As Magnus O'Meere, he sat out by the tree.
Right then an idea came into his sight
That instantly brought him tremendous delight...

Off he went to invent some giggle robotics
With his stockpile of parts and Dad's old orthotics.
He worked right through recess and gave it his best
Then raced back to class and put it to the test.

His teacher, Miss Richter,
    he found was a stickler.
She was quite unimpressed
    with his motorized tickler.

"Mr. Magnus O'Meere, your newest attraction
Is proving to be an outrageous distraction.
Please go put it away. Now, what did I say?
You've got to get focused; it's not time to play."

Then Miss Richter gave out, to each lad and lass,
A task to prepare and present to the class.
A project she loved; one designed to inspire:

HISTORIC HERO PROJECT

"Research a hero
that you fondly admire."

Magnus tried to stay focused,

but, try as he might,

His mind wandered off on a perilous flight...

Riding a rocket—staring off into space,
Distraction was written all over his face.

"Focus please."

His breakthrough idea was right on the brim,
So, Magnus O'Meere, he went out on a whim...

Stewing solutions—
   no, he just couldn't quit.
Then he stood up and shouted,
   "Eureka, that's it!"

"Mr. Magnus O'Meere,
   you can't pay attention.
I've had it to here, now
   you're off to detention."

His mother was most unenthused with the news,
Which left Magnus feeling a little confused.

His heart hit the floor—he felt so deflated.
He started to question the things he'd created.

Magnus served his detention deep in the library.
But his consequence there was quite the contrary.

A
book **fell**
on
his
head

by a sheer stroke of fate.

And
delivered
a
message

he couldn't debate.

Magnus learned that Tesla was one-of-a-kind.
He built perfect inventions deep down in his mind.
Enthralled with Einstein, his fascination grew on...

Captivated, he studied them out on the lawn.

Spellbound by da Vinci

and dazzled by Musk,

He explored masterful minds

until it was dusk.

Then Magnus lit up
as it all became clear.
"This is what I've been doing
for all of these years!"

He began meditation to
perfect how to find
The space to build ideas
deep in his mind.

With practice, he found which spots had grown rusted
And located where projects must be adjusted.

With dedication, his minds were able to merge
To perfect epic visions that were stuck on the verge.
He hit many roadblocks, but by taking a shower,
Solutions emerged with an awe-striking power.

Magnus blew minds as he presented in class
A pioneer view through a new looking glass.

Einstein used intuition,
    then backed it with knowledge.
His "mind experiments"
    were not learned in college.

ALBERT EINSTEIN

NIKOLA TESLA

Both Tesla and Henry
    envisioned inventions
With precision that was
    beyond comprehension.

BEULAH LOUISE HENRY

"These marvellous minds utilized intuition
To impact the world with creative ambition."

WOLFGANG MOZART

Mozart played pool while
he divinely designed
Great symphonies that
he refined in his mind.

STEPHANIE KWOLEK

Kwolek was a chemist
who trusted her hunches
To create concoctions that
withstood the "punches."

THOMAS EDISON

Edison sat in a chair
in front of a fire
To induce the brain-state
he dearly desired.

"Why don't we meditate to dive into our minds
Where boundless ideas sit and wait to unwind?"

He gave guided direction to help his friends learn
How to find inspiration and get it to churn.

Miss Richter was beaming—she was smiling and proud.
"You focused your mind; brought it down from the clouds.
You have taught me so much!" she freely confessed,
"I must say, young man, I am wildly impressed."

Have an inquiring mind and make your own rules.
Many mind pioneers were once thought to be fools.

But they shattered the limits and blazed their own trails.
You can't change the world if you're too scared to fail.

So, find what excites you, then follow the thread,
And do keep a notebook right next to your bed.

Now, go choose a topic that lights up your heart,
Envision your dreams and begin on your start.

Meditate
to find inspiration
+
Choose a topic
that excites you
+
Envision your dreams
+
Begin on your start!

Magnus harnessed his mind and unwavering might
To fuel his ideas and help them take flight.

He gave it his all, and with meticulous care,
Pioneered new inventions—ambitious and rare.

Marvellous Minds Guide

Italian painter, sculptor, inventor, architect, and military engineer who was centuries ahead of his time. Creator of the aerial screw, self-propelled cart, Mona Lisa, and more.

Mind Hack: Whole-brain thinking; sketched ideas, inspiration, detailed observation; poly-phasic sleep.

Leonardo da Vinci

English physicist, mathematician, astronomer, theologian, and author who developed Newton's Laws of Motion.

Mind Hack: Held focus on a problem in his mind until he could see through it to the solution.

Sir Isaac Newton

Austrian-born musical prodigy who created over 600 classical music compositions. Mozart wrote his first symphony at the age of 8 years old.

Mind Hack: Played pool while composing music in his mind.

Wolfgang Mozart

British mathematician and writer, considered the first computer programmer in the 18th century.

Mind Hack: Used intuition and imagination to apply mathematical and scientific concepts.

Ada Lovelace

American inventor and businessman with over 1,000 patents including the phonograph and the practical light bulb.

Mind Hack: Relaxed in front of a fire while holding ball bearings in his hands; they would fall to the floor to wake him if he fell asleep.

Thomas Edison

Serbian-American inventor, mechanical and electrical engineer, and futurist with over 300 patents including the AC motor and many electrical inventions.

Mind Hack: Mind journeys; long walks; envisioned, built, and tested inventions intuitively in his mind.

Nikola Tesla

German-born theoretical physicist who developed the Theory of Relativity, e=MC2 equation, and the Law of the Photoelectric Effect.

Mind Hack: Thought experiments, mind journeys, listened to music, and thought in images and feelings.

Albert Einstein

American self-taught engineer and inventor of 110 inventions including the vacuum ice cream freezer.

Mind Hack: Activated subtle senses, trusted her instincts, and visualized the devices she wanted to make in her mind.

Beulah Louise Henry

Indian mathematician, from the early 1900s, who made substantial contributions, while having almost no formal training in mathematics.

Mind Hack: Answers fell into his mind while meditating and praying.

Srinivasa Ramanujan

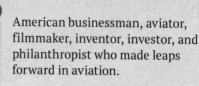

American businessman, aviator, filmmaker, inventor, investor, and philanthropist who made leaps forward in aviation.

Mind Hack: Intuitively acted on decisions that felt right, followed his inspiration, and thought big.

Howard Hughes

Mind Hack: A technique that opens the mind to get "in the zone" where ideas, creativity, intuition, and peak performance flow with ease.

Hedy Lamarr

Austrian-born actress and inventor of frequency-hopping technology that formed the basis for wifi and bluetooth. Revolutionized airplane wing design.

Mind Hack: Invented as a destressor, followed her tinkering passion, and trusted her ideas.

Jonas Salk

American medical researcher and virologist who invented one of the first successful polio vaccines.

Mind Hack: Merged reason with intuition; visualized being the virus and the immune system, to better understand the disease he was researching.

Stephanie Kwolek

American chemist who is the inventor of Kevlar—a strong material used in bulletproof vests.

Mind Hack: Whole-brain thinking; looked further into mixtures that seemed to not work out at first.

Stephen Hawking

English theoretical physicist, cosmologist, and author who coined the theory of Hawking Radiation.

Mind Hack: Used mental images and diagrams, took intuitive leaps, and visualized winding back the clock to the beginning of time.

Temple Grandin

American inventor, professor of animal science, and autism spokesperson.

Mind Hack: Runs full-motion equipment testing in her imagination, bottom-up thinking, and thinks in pictures.

Steve Jobs

American technology entrepreneur, business magnate, and co-founder of Apple. Recognized as a co-pioneer of the microcomputer revolution.

Mind Hack: Scheduled technology-free time, intuitive meditation, and mindfulness for laser-like focus.

J.K. Rowling

British novelist, screenwriter, and producer of the Harry Potter empire.

Mind Hack: Gives structure to her vivid imagination by organizing and sketching her ideas.

Elon Musk

South-African born engineer, tech entrepreneur, and innovative genius. Founder of SpaceX, SolarCity, and co-founder of Tesla Motors.

Mind Hack: First-principle analysis, never-ending inquiries, avid reading, big thinking, and laser-like focus.

Tiger Woods

American professional golf legend who holds numerous golf records.

Mind Hack: Employs mental imagery and visualization to enhance his golf game, utilizes a mental swing routine, and mentally rehearses challenging scenarios.

Serena Williams

American world-class tennis champion with over 20 Grand slam singles and multiple Olympic gold medals.

Mind Hack: Uses mental imagery and visualization to enhance performance.

Reflection Questions

"Reading without reflecting is like eating without digesting."
-Edmund Burke

Magnus O'Meere is a brave Mind Pioneer. He loves solving problems
and thinking outside-the-box to come up with creative ideas.
What big ideas would you like to invent, create, dream, or do?

Not everyone thinks or learns in the same way.
Magnus didn't realize that his big imagination and creative
thinking abilities were truly his own unique super powers.
What unique super power do you possess?

Was there ever a time where getting in trouble or facing an
obstacle made you question your desires and talents or made
you want to give up on an idea? What did you do?
How could you find inspiration to keep blazing your own trail?

When the book of inventors fell on Magnus' head, it was a perfect
moment of synchronicity—it happened for him, and at the exact moment
he needed it. Have you ever had something happen, with such
perfect timing, that you knew it was a sign—just for you?

Have you ever had trouble focusing your mind
What did you do to overcome that?

What if, instead of viewing problems as obstacles, we could
see them as opportunities to grow and learn? What was the
last obstacle you had to face? What did you learn from it?
What would you do differently, if it happened again?

Magnus was blown away with what he discovered in those library books.
Have you ever had an exciting insight or idea that made something
make perfect sense? What sparked this insight for you?

Books are a great way to learn, grow, and reflect.
What are some other ways you could expand your
mind and allow your ideas to take flight?

By focusing his mind, Magnus was able to turn his passion into an
empowering career where he could make a difference. What wild dreams
would you go after, if you found that place in your mind for ideas to unwind?

*For FREE imagination-inducing learning activities for the Mind Pioneers in
your life, visit our website at www.InnerCompassBooks.com/learning-resource

About the Author

Photo by Nancy Newby Photography

Like Magnus O'Meere, Kristin Pierce became fascinated with the intuitive power of the mind. With years of practice, she now utilizes her intuition to create

Kristin Pierce is an award-winning author, the founder of Inner Compass Books, and a self-awareness educator whose mission is to empower others to deconstruct their self-limiting beliefs, shift their perspectives, open their minds, and expand their awareness of mind, body, and self. It is her mission to create mindfully-crafted children's books that encourage kids to question their limits, pursue their passions, and dream bigger than belief.

Kristin lives in Saskatchewan, Canada with her husband, two children, and their dog.

Magnus O'Meere, Mind Pioneer is her third children's book.

Other Titles from Inner Compass Books:

For FREE learning resources, visit **www.InnerCompassBooks.com** and find Inner Compass Books on Facebook and Instagram @InnerCompassBooks.

Dedication:

For the first Mind Pioneers I ever witnessed in action—my twin brothers, Kenton and Kiel.

And for my little Mind Pioneers, Aspen and Kendrix—always
remember that you can do anything you set your mind to.

Note from the Author:

Magnus O'Meere, Mind Pioneer was created to honour the courageous mind pioneers
throughout history whose bravery, imaginations, ideas, and innovations have boldly
impacted the world. It is my hope that this book educates and inspires future generations
to unlock the power of their minds and make their own mark—because we ALL have the
ability to create change in the world by harnessing the potential of our minds.

Acknowledgements:

I would like to thank my husband for his patience and support in being my sounding board and enduring
my never-ending (and sometimes one-sided) conversations that come with any project I set out to create.
I'd also like to extend a big thank you to Lacy Lieffers for her editing expertise and guidance along
the way. Gratitude goes out to Mar Fandos for sticking with me to bring this project to life. And lastly,
thank you to my husband, kids, friends, family, and readers for their support and encouragement.

Edited by: Lacy Lieffers of One Leaf Editing
Title design by: Matt Pierce
Art direction, book layout, and cover design by: Kristin Pierce
Invention and artwork idea contributions by: Aspen Pierce, Matt Pierce, and Kendrix Pierce

Magnus O'Meere, Mind Pioneer
Copyright © 2019 by Kristin Pierce

ISBN
978-1-99908-810-1 (Hardcover)
978-1-99908-811-8 (Paperback)

Inner Compass
Books.com

Find us on Facebook and Instagram @
InnerCompassBooks, and stay tuned
for more book magic coming your way.

CPSIA information can be obtained
at www.ICGtesting.com
Printed in the USA
LVHW071643161121
703499LV00006B/274

9 781999 088101